建设美丽西安

Constructing a Beautiful Xi'an

2013 西安概览

2013 A SURVEY OF XI'AN

顾　　问／魏民洲
主　　编／吕　健
副 主 编／王德安　郝小奇
编　　辑／孙怀国　赵群洁　刘　健　张小军
　　　　　凌高峰　曹晓雷　唐艳艳　何　荔
执行编辑／吴瀛栋
设　　计／王　锋
翻　　译／郭熙玲
鸣　　谢／西安市外办　西安市统计局

《西安赋》
Ode of Xi'an

[城阙辅三秦，雄立千秋曾聚天下王气；河岳壮九州，名扬四海折腰无数英雄，是为长治久安之福地，贵有龙凤呈祥之鼎盛。]

——《光明日报》「百城赋」首篇。

Vast Guanzhong Plain Safeguards the Ancient Chang'an City,
Which Serves as the Capitals of Great Dynasties for Thousands of Years.
Magnificence of the Rivers and Mountains outstands the land of China, Fascinating Innumerable Heroes and People of Visions,
Being a Splendid Land of Permanent Peace, Stability and Prosperity.

——Odes of Hundred Cities, Guangming Daily

建设国际化大都市,是国家对西安发展的新定位,是省委、省政府对西安发展的新要求,是市第十二次党代会作出的新部署,更是全市人民的新期盼。我们各项工作要始终紧盯这一目标不放松、不动摇,加快建设具有历史文化特色的国际化大都市步伐。

——摘自中共陕西省委常委、西安市委书记魏民洲在市委十二届二次全会第二次全体会议上的讲话

Building Xi'an into an international metropolis is a new direction set by the State Government, a new requirement of the CPC Shaanxi Provincial Committee and Shaanxi Provincial Government, a new blueprint drawn by the 12th Municipal Party Congress, moreover, a new anticipation of all people in Xi'an. We shall faithfully adhere to this goal and accelerate the construction of International Metropolis with historic and cultural features.

——Selected from the speech of Mr Wei Minzhou, Member of the CPC Shaanxi Provincial Standing Committee, Party Secretary of the CPC Xi'an Municipal Committee, in the 2nd Plenary Meeting of the 12th CPC Municipal Committee.

渭北工业区建设、汉长安城遗址保护、秦岭北麓生态环境建设、"八水润西安"工程和公路交通枢纽建设,是我市着眼长远、重点推进的五项重点工作。我们一定要举全市之力,攻坚克难,狠抓落实,努力实现新起点上的新跨越。

——摘自市委副书记、市长董军在西安市第十五届人大三次会议上的政府工作报告

Special focus and full efforts shall be given to the 5 key tasks namely Weibei Industrial Zone Construction, Heritage Protection of Han Chang'an City, Eco-environmental Protection of the North Foot of Qingling Mountain, the Project of Eight Rivers Nourishing Xi'an and Road Transportation Hub Construction. We shall overcome any possible difficulties with great determination and motivation to carry forward our work to a new height.

——Selected from the Government Work Report by Mr Dong Jun, Deputy Party Secretary of the CPC Xi'an Municipal Committee, Mayor of Xi'an, in the 3rd Session of the 15th Municipal People's Congress.

目录
Contents

综合实力   11
Comprehensive Power

西安概况   16
Xi'an Survey

历史沿革   21
Contemporary History

经济结构   26
Economic Structure

农业经济   33
Agricultural Economy

现代工业   36
Modern Industry

第三产业   38
Tertiary Industry

城市建设   44
Urban Construction

西安概览 2013 A SURVEY OF XI AN

对外开放 Opening to the Outside World	49
人民生活 People's livelihood	52
科技教育 Science, Technology and Education	55
社会事业 Social Undertakings	60
名胜古迹 Historic Monuments	63
开发区建设 Construction of Development Zones	72
区县概况 Districts and Counties	80
前景目标 Prospects and Targets	88

市树: 国槐
City Tree: Chinese Scholar Tree

市花: 石榴花
City Flower: Pomegranate Flower

名人说西安

要走进中国,只有从西安才能进入。

——克林顿

中国四大文明,三个与西安有关。

——文怀沙

长安寻梦,愿西安模式在探索中成为现实。

——吴良镛

古城无价宝,科学难再造,继承与发展,保护最重要。

——周干峙

西安不是一个随便就可以写的城市。

——余秋雨

Remarks by Elites

Xi'an is the way leading to China.   ------- Bill Clinton

Three out of the four civilizations created by China are related to Xi'an.   ------Wen Huaisha

Return back to Chang'an in the dream. May Xi'an model turn into reality in the process of exploration.   ------Wu Liangyong

The invaluable ancient city can hardly be recreated by scientific means. Protection is the key issue in balancing inheritance and development.   ------Zhou Ganshi

Xi'an cannot be accurately described without adequate knowledge.

------Yu Qiuyu

西安市荣获的荣誉称号

西安市先后荣获国家卫生城市、国家园林城市、全国创建文明城市工作先进城市、国际著名旅游目的地城市、中国十佳最具软实力城市、2009中国最具幸福感城市、建设创新型国家十强市、2011年全国十大创新型城市、中国服务外包示范城市、十大中国最关爱民生城市、全国节水型社会建设示范市、中国国际形象最佳城市、中国十佳绿色城市、全国创业先进城市等荣誉称号和2010物流中心城市杰出成就奖。连续七次获得全国双拥模范城荣誉称号；连续三届被评为全国社会治安综合治理优秀城市，荣获全国社会治安综合治理最高奖项"长安杯"。

Honors Awarded to Xi'an

National Hygienic City, National Garden City, National Civilized City, World-Renowned Tourism Destination, Top Ten Competitive City, One of the Chinese Cities Best Satisfied to the Happiness of Citizens in 2009, Top Ten National Innovative City, Top Ten National Innovative City 2011, China Business Outsourcing Model City, Top Ten National City for Taking Care of Citizen's Livelihood, National Model City for Water-Saving, Top National City for International Image, Top Ten National Green City, Top National City for Establishing Business, 2010 Outstanding Central City for Logistics, National Model City for Taking Care of Those Who Lost Their Family Members in the Service of Our Country (6 times), National Public Security Model City(3 times); Being Awarded " Chang'an Cup", National Top Prize for Public Security.

综合实力
Comprehensive Power

2012年西安市主要经济指标完成情况
Main Economic Index for 2012

2008年–2012年西安市主要经济指标
Main Economic Index for 2008-2012

西安概览

2013 A SURVEY OF XI'AN

2012年西安市主要经济指标完成情况

- 地区生产总值4369.37亿元，增长11.8%
- 规模以上工业增加值1144.29亿元，增长13.0%
- 全社会固定资产投资4243.43亿元，增长26.6%
- 社会消费品零售总额2236.06亿元，增长15.5%
- 地方财政一般预算收入396.96亿元，增长24.6%
- 进出口总额130.14亿美元，增长3.3%
- 城镇居民人均可支配收入29982元，增长15.4%
- 农村居民人均纯收入11442元，增长16.9%

Main Economic Index for 2012

- GDP reached 436.937 billion yuan, increased by11.8% .
- Added value for above-scale industries reached 114.429 billion yuan, increased by 13.0%.
- Investment for social fixed assets came to 424.343 billion yuan, increased by 26.6% year-on year.
- Total volume of retail sales of social consumption came to 223.606 billion yuan, increased by 15.5%.
- Local revenue came to 39.696 billion yuan, increased by 24.6% .
- Import and export volume reached 13.014 billion USD, increased by 3.3%.
- Per Capita disposable income for urban residents amounted to 29982 yuan, increased by 15.4% .
- Net income for rural residents amounted to 11442 yuan, increased by 16.9%.

2008年-2012年西安市主要经济指标

Main Economic Index for 2008-2012

地区生产总值（亿元）
GDP (RMB 100 million Yuan)

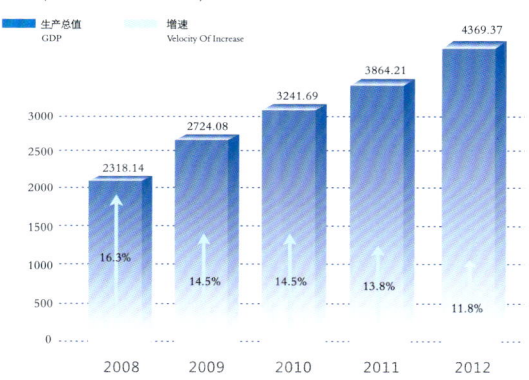

规模以上工业增加值（亿元）
Added value for above-scale industries (RMB 100 million Yuan)

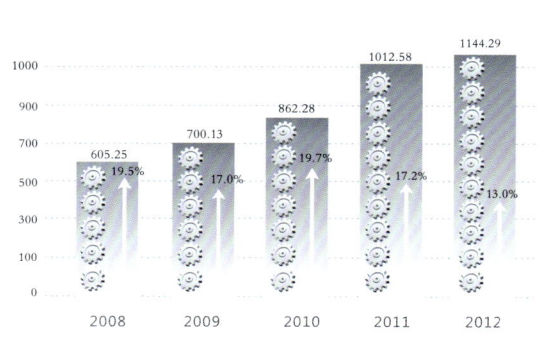

全社会固定资产投资（亿元）
Investment for social fixed assets (RMB 100 million Yuan)

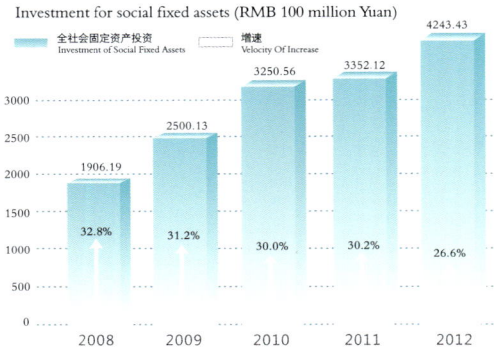

社会消费品零售总额（亿元）
Retail sales for social consumption (RMB 100 million Yuan)

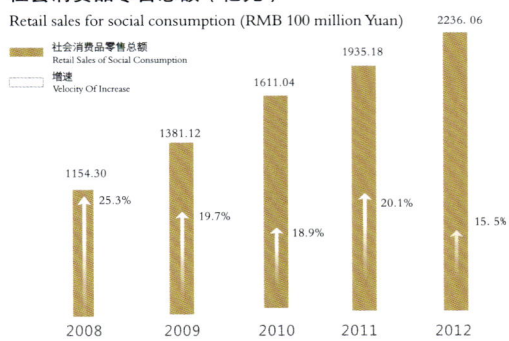

地方财政一般预算收入（亿元）
Local revenue (RMB 100 million Yuan)

进出口总额（亿美元）
Import and Export Volume (100 million dollars)

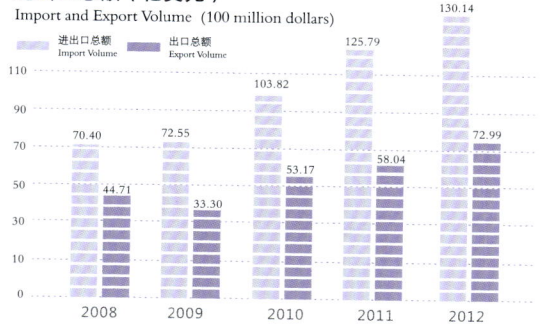

城镇居民可支配收入（元）
Per Capita disposable income for urban residents (RMB Yuan)

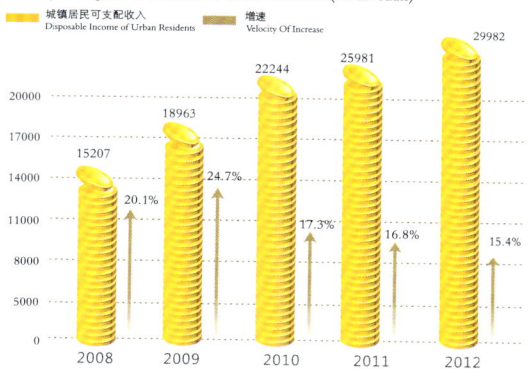

农村居民人均纯收入（元）
Net income for rural residents (RMB Yuan)

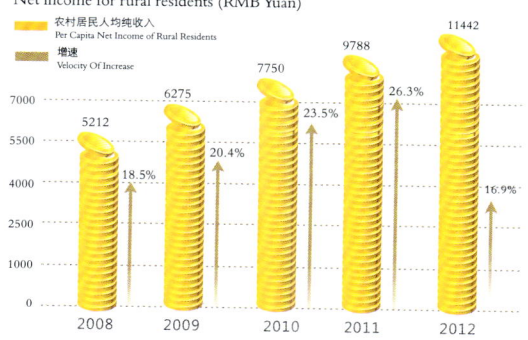

西安概况
Xi'an Survey

市情概况
Brief Introduction of Xi'an

自然地理
Nature and Geography

物产资源
Natural Resources

市情概况

西安古称长安，是中华民族和人类文明的重要发祥地之一，是陕西省省会，国家重要的科研、教育和工业基地，我国西部地区重要的中心城市，世界历史文化名城，具有3100多年建城史和1100多年建都史，是与雅典、罗马、开罗齐名的世界著名历史古都。

西安现辖新城、碑林、莲湖、雁塔、灞桥、未央、阎良、临潼、长安9个区，蓝田、周至、户县、高陵4个县（共有109个街道、67个镇、782个社区和2991个行政村），有国家级西安高新技术产业开发区、国家级西安经济技术开发区、西安曲江新区、西安浐灞生态区、西安阎良国家航空高技术产业基地、西安国家民用航天产业基地、西安国际港务区和西安沣东新城（简称"五区一港两基地"）。总面积10108平方公里，市区规划面积865平方公里，截至2012年底，主城区建成区面积449平方公里。

2009年6月，国务院批复的《关中—天水经济区发展规划》明确提出：着力打造西安国际化大都市，到2020年都市区人口发展到1000万人以上，主城区面积达到800平方公里。

Brief Introduction of Xi'an

Known as Chang'an in ancient times, Xi'an is the cradle of Chinese nation and human civilization. Being the capital of Shaanxi province, Xi'an serves as an important national base for science and technology, education and industry, a central city in west China and a famed historical and cultural city. Xi'an takes pride in her 3,100-year-old city history and 1,100-year-old capital history. It is a world-renowned ancient capital that shares the same prestige with Athens, Rome and Cairo.

Xi'an has 9 districts under its jurisdiction, namely Xincheng, Beilin, Lianhu, Yanta, Baqiao, Weiyang, Yanliang, Lintong and Chang'an, as well as 4 counties namely Lantian, Zhouzhi, Huxian and Gaoling (with 109 streets, 67 towns, 782 communities and 2991 administrative villages). 8 development zones have taken shape in Xi'an, namely, the National Xi'an High-tech Industries Development Zone, the National Xi'an Economic and Technological Development Zone, Yanliang National Aviation High-tech Industrial Base, Xi'an National Civil Aerospace Industrial Base, Qujiang New District, Chanhe&Bahe Rivers Ecological Zone, Xi'an International Trade & Logistics Zone, Xi'an Fengwei New Area. Xi'an covers an area of 10,108 km². Out of 865 km² urban area under city planning , 395 km² main urban area has been configured by the end of 2010.

Guanzhong—Tianshui Economic Belt Development Plan authorized by the State Council in June 2009 clearly stated: build Xi'an into an international metropolis with urban population of 10 million and main urban area of 800 km² by 2020.

自然地理

西安地处黄河流域中部的关中平原，中国地理版图中心。东西长约204公里，南北宽约116公里，平均海拔424米，境内最高点为周至县西南的太白山，海拔3867米。西安属暖温带半湿润的季风气候，四季分明，雨热同期，日光充足，自然环境优越。年平均气温15.5℃，降水约600mm，湿度69.6%，日照1377小时。

Nature and Geography

Nestled in the Central Shaanxi Plain around the middle reach of Yellow River and located at the geological center of Chinese territory, Xi'an spans 204 km from east to west and 116 km from north to south. The average altitude is 424 m, with the summit found in the 3,867-meter-high Mount Taibai in the southwest Zhouzhi County. Situated in the temperate zone and featuring semi-humid monsoon climate, Xi'an has distinctive four seasons with rainfalls concentrated in hot season. The city is blessed with mild climate, ample sunshine and favorable natural environment. The annual temperature averages 15.5℃, precipitation near 600 mm, humidity around 69.6% and sunlight adding up to 1,377 hours.

物产资源

西安素有"八水绕长安"之说，灞、浐、沣、涝、潏、滈、泾、渭八条河流绕城而过，灌溉条件便利，农业生产条件得天独厚，农作物、林木、畜禽种类繁多，秦川牛和关中驴享有盛誉。

西安动植物资源丰富，列为国家保护的一类珍稀动物3种，二类保护动物4种。境内有自然保护区6处，保护面积147.96万亩，野生植物138科、681属、2224种，其中经济价值较高的有1200余种，是我国种子植物的重要"基因

库"之一。

西安有各类矿产资源54种,已开发利用24种,优势矿产主要有黄金、建材类非金属等。

Natural Resources

Having been described as "a city with eight rivers flowing around" (namely Bahe River, Chanhe River, Fenghe River, Laohe River,Yuhe River, Haohe River, Jinghe River and Weihe River), Xi'an enjoys complete irrigation system, creating favorable conditions for agriculture. There are many varieties of farm products, trees, livestock and poultry, among which Qinchuan cattle and central Shaanxi donkey are most famous.

Xi'an is rich in animal and plant resources. 3 species of animals are rated to be first-class rare animals under state protection while 4 species are rated to be second-class ones. Xi'an has established 6 natural reserves with a total area covering 1.4796 million mu(1 mu=1/15 hectares). Wild plants in Xi'an fall into 138 families, 681 genera and 2,224 species, 1,200 species of which have high economic value. It is one of the important Gene Pools for seed plants in China.

Xi'an is home to 54 kinds of minerals, 24 kinds of which having been excavated and utilized. Valuable minerals include gold and nonmetallic building materials.

历史沿革
Contemporary History

西安之名由来
Origin of the City's Name

历史沿革
Contemporary History

13朝古都
Capital City of 13 Dynasties

西安概览

2013 A SURVEY OF XI'AN

西安之名由来

西安,在公元前1046年的西周时称"丰镐",是周文王和周武王分别修建的中国历史上第一个全国性的国家政权的首都"丰京"和"镐京"的合称。西汉初年(公元前206年),刘邦定都西安,称"长安",意思为"长治久安",此后至唐朝末年(公元907年),长安作为中国古代十三个王朝的首都一直沿用了1100多年。唐朝灭亡后,西安还先后被称为京兆府(后唐)、陕西路(宋)、安西路(元)、奉元路(元)等,是中国西北地区的政治、经济、文化中心。1369年明朝建立后的第二年春天,明朝皇帝朱元璋的大将徐达攻下奉元路,将奉元路改名为"西安",意思是安定西北。从此,西安的名称一直沿用至今。

Origin of the City's Name

As far back as 1,046 B.C, the first nationwide political authority in China was founded by Zhou Wenwang and Zhou Wuwang of Western Zhou dynasty, setting up the capital in Fenghao(today's Xi'an). During the early period of Western Han dynasty in 206 B.C, Liu Bang set up capital in Chang'an(today's Xi'an), carrying the meaning of eternal peace. The name of capital Chang'an lasted 1,100 years until 907 A.D in late Tang dynasty. After the doom of Tang dynasty, Xi'an was renamed Jingzhao Fu(in Later Tang dynasty), Shaanxi Lu（in Song dynasty）, Anxi lu and Fengyuan Lu(in Yuan dynasty) and had played the role of a political, economic and cultural center in the northwest region of China. In the spring of 1369, the year after Ming dynasty was established, emperor Zhu Yuanzhang sent general Xuda to conquer Fengyuan Lu and changed the city's name into Xi'an, carrying the meaning of stability in the northwest region. The name lasted up till today.

历史沿革

1949年5月20日西安解放。建国后，西安曾是中央西北局和西北行政委员会所在地，中央人民政府的直辖市；1954年改为省辖市，1984年恢复计划单列，1992年被批准为内陆开放城市；1994年被批准为全国综合配套改革试点城市和副省级城市。经过60多年的建设和发展，西安已形成门类较为齐全的工业体系和城市服务体系，成为我国重要的科研、高等教育、国防科技工业和高新技术产业基地及辐射中西部地区的金融、科技、教育、旅游、商贸中心。

Contemporary History

May 20, 1949 celebrated the liberation of the Xi'an city. Upon the founding of the People's Republic of China, Xi'an was chosen as the headquarter for the Northwest Bureau of the Central Committee of the CPC and the Northwest Administrative Committee respectively and a city directly under the jurisdiction of the Central Government. In 1954, it turned to be the capital city of Shaanxi Province and was listed under separate state planning in 1984. In 1992, it was approved as an opening city of inland China. In 1994, Xi'an was authorized to be the national comprehensive supporting reform pilot city and a sub-provincial city. Having undergone over more than 60 years of development, a complete industrial system and urban service system have taken shape. Xi'an has become the key scientific research, higher education, national defense and hi-tech industrial base in China. It also plays the role of a hub of finance, science and technology, education, tourism, and trade in the mid-western region of Northern China.

13朝古都

历史上曾有西周、秦、西汉、新、东汉、西晋、前赵、前秦、后秦、西魏、北周、隋、唐等13个朝代在西安建都。

西安作为历代首都共计1129年。

Capital City of 13 Dynasties

Historically, 13 dynasties had established their capitals in Xi'an, including West Zhou Dynasty, Qin Dynasty, West Han Dynasty, Xin Dynasty, East Han Dynasty (Emperor Xian), West Jin Dynasty (Emperor Min), Former Zhao, Former Qin, Later Qin Dynasty, West Wei Dynasty, North Zhou Dynasty, Sui Dynasty and Tang Dynasty.

The time span of Xi'an serving as Chinese ancient capital adds up to 1,129years.

附：曾在西安建都朝代及历时统计表

Note: Chronological List of Xi'an-based Dynasties

朝代 Dynasty	首都名称 Name of Capital	首都地点 Location	始止年份 Year of Starting and Ending	前后历时 Tenure (years)
西周 West Zhou	丰镐 Fenghao	西安市 长安区境 Chang'an District	武王元年（公元前1046年） 至幽王十一年（公元前771） The 49th year of Emperor Wu (1046 B.C.) The 1st year of Emperor You (770 B.C.)	276
秦 Qin	栎阳 Yueyang	西安市 阎良区境 Yanliang District	秦献公二年（公元前383年） 至孝公十二年（公元前350年） The 12th year of Emperor Xiangong(383 B.C.) The 12th year of Emperor Xiangong(350 B.C.)	178
	咸阳 Xianyang	西安市 未央区境 Weiyang District	秦孝公十二年 至子婴元年（公元前206年） The 12th year of Emperor Xiangong The 1st year of Emperor Xiangong(206 B.C.)	
西汉 West Han	长安 Chang'an	西安市 未央区境 Weiyang District	汉高祖元年（公元前206年） 至孺子初始一年（公元8年） The 1st year of Emperor Gaozu (206B.C.) The 1st year of Emperor Ruzi (8 A.D.)	214
新 Xin	长安 Chang'an	西安市 未央区境 Weiyang District	王莽始建国元年（公元9年） 至地皇四年（公元23年） The 1st year of Wangmang (9 A.D.) The 4th year of Emperor Dihuang (23 A.D.)	15
东汉（献帝） East Han Dynasty (Emperor Xian)	长安 Chang'an	西安市 未央区境 Weiyang District	东汉初平元年（公元190年） 至兴平五年（公元195年） The 1st year of Emperor Chuping (190 A.D.) The 5th year of Emperor Xingping (195 A.D.)	6
西晋（愍帝） West Jin Dynasty (Emperor Min)	长安 Chang'an	西安市 未央区境 Weiyang District	西晋建兴元年（公元313年） 至建兴四年（公元316年） The 1st year (313 A.D.) to the 4th year of Emperor Jianxing (316 A.D.)	4
前赵 Former Zhao	长安 Chang'an	西安市 未央区境 Weiyang District	前赵光初二年（公元319年） 至光初十二年（公元329年） The 2nd year (319 A.D.) to the 12th year of Emperor Guangchu (329 A.D.)	11
前秦 Former Qin	长安 Chang'an	西安市 未央区境 Weiyang District	前秦始皇元年（公元351年） 至太安元年（公元385年） The 1st year of Emperor Shihuang (351 A.D.) The 1st year of Emperor Taian (385 A.D.)	35
后秦 Later Qin	长安 Chang'an	西安市 未央区境 Weiyang District	后秦建初元年（公元386年） 至永和二年（公元417年） The 1st year of Emperor Jianchu (386 A.D.) The 2nd year of Emperor Yonghe (417 A.D.)	32
西魏 West Wei	长安 Chang'an	西安市 未央区境 Weiyang District	西魏大统元年（公元535年） 至恭帝三年（公元557年） The 3rd year of Emperor Datong (535 A.D.) The 4th year of Emperor Gong (557 A.D.)	23
北周 North Zhou	长安 Chang'an	西安市 未央区境 Weiyang District	北周孝闵帝一年（公元557年） 至大定一年（公元581年） The 1st year of Emperor Xiaomin (557 A.D.) The 1st year of Emperor Dading (581 A.D.)	25
隋 Sui	大兴 Daxing	西安市市区 Xi'an city	隋开皇元年（公元581年） 至大业十四年（公元618年） The 1st year of Emperor Kaihuang (581 A.D.) The 14th year of Emperor Daye (618 A.D.)	38
唐 Tang	长安 Chang'an	西安市市区 Xi'an city	唐武德元年（公元618年） 至天授元年（公元690年） The 1st year of Emperor Wude (618 A.D.) The 1st year of Emperor Tianshou (690 A.D.)	272
	长安 Chang'an	西安市市区 Xi'an city	唐神龙元年（公元705年） 至天佑四年（公元904年） The 1st year of Emperor Shenlong (705 A.D.) The 4th year of Emperor Tianyou (904 A.D.)	
合计 Total				1129

产业结构
Industrial Structure

就业结构
Employment Structure

所有制结构
Ownership Structure

五大主导产业
Five Pillar Industries

五项重点工作
Five Key Tasks

经济结构
Economic Structure

产业结构

2012年，第一产业完成增加值195.59亿元，增长6.0%；第二产业完成增加值1893.79亿元，增长11.8%；第三产业完成增加值2279.99亿元，增长12.2%。

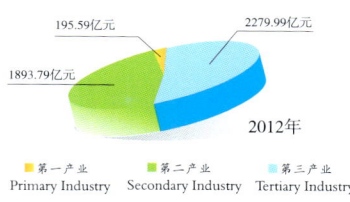

Industrial Structure

In 2012, Primary industry achieved an increment of 19.559 billion yuan, a 6.0% growth. The secondary industry realized an increment of 189.379 billion yuan, a 11.8% growth. The tertiary industry achieved an increase of 227.999 billion yuan, a 12.2% growth.

就业结构

2012年，全市从业人员中，第一产业从业人员为123.83万人，第二产业从业人员为156.35万人，第三产业从业人员为230.07万人，三次产业从业人员比例为24.3：30.6：45.1。

Employment Structure

In 2012, 1.2383 million employers served for primary industry, 1.5635 million employers served for secondary industry while 2.3007 million employers served for tertiary industry. The proportion of the employers served for above-mentioned three industries amounted to 24.3:30.6:45.1.

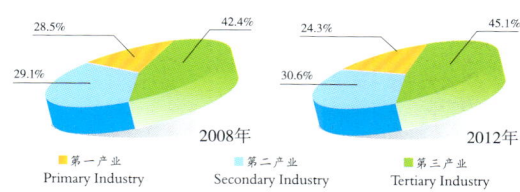

所有制结构

2012年,非公有制经济增加值完成2245.75亿元,是2008年的2倍,占GDP比重为51.4%,较2008年提高3.8个百分点。

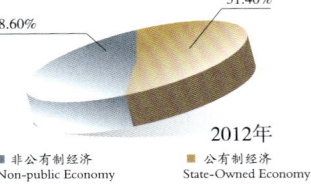

■ 非公有制经济　　■ 公有制经济
Non-public Economy　　State-Owned Economy

Ownership Structure

In 2012, the added value of non-public economy counted up to 224.575 billion yuan, 2 times than that of 2008, 51.4% of the whole GDP growth, 3.8% higher than that seen in 2008.

五大主导产业

Five Pillar Industries

2012年五大主导产业增加值
2012 Absolute Value for Five Pillar Industries

产业类别 Category	2012年完成情况(亿元) 2012 Absolute Value for Five Pillar Industries (100 million yuan)	占GDP比重(%) Proportion to GDP
地区生产总值 GDP of Xi'an	4369.37	—
高新技术产业 High-tech	510.82	11.7
装备制造业 Equipment Manufacturing	684.21	15.7
旅游业 Tourism	385.03	8.8
文化产业 Culture	334.68	7.7
现代服务业 Modern Service	1428.08	32.7
五大主导产业增加值 (剔除重复)合计 Absolute Value for Five Pillar Industries (repetition excluded)	2276.38	52.1

五项重点工作

Five Key Tasks

渭北工业区建设。 2012年7月6日,市委常委会通过了《渭北工业区规划》,8月16日正式挂牌启动,远期规划851平方公里,一期建设213平方公里,突出发展先进制造业和战略性新兴产业,重

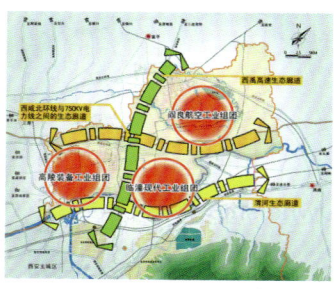

点打造高陵装备工业、阎良航空工业、临潼现代工业三个组团。力争到2015年,渭北工业区工业总产值达到1800亿元,工业增加值达到500亿元。

Weibei Industrial Zone. In 6th July, 2012, the Standing Committee of the CPC Xi'an Municipal Committee has approved The Master Plan of Weibei Industrial Zone and officially launched the project on 16th August. With long-term planned area as large as 851 km², 213km² out of which will be completed in the first phase, Weibei Industrial Zone highlights the advanced manufacturing and strategic emerging industry, aims to create a new economic growth pole featuring Gaoling equipment industry, Yanliang aviation industry and Lintong Modern Industry. Efforts will be devoted to make the total industrial output value of Weibei Industrial Zone reached 180 billion Yuan and industrial value-added 50 billion Yuan by 2015.

汉长安城遗址保护。2012年8月3日,市委常委会通过了《西安汉长安城国家大遗址保护特区实施方案》,成立了建设领导小组和管委会,明确了建设主体单位,全面启动36平方公里遗址保护建设。今年将完成遗址区内本体保护工程展示和水系、路网等基础设施建设,6月通过申遗验收,7月底前未央宫前殿遗址公园开园。

Heritage Protection of Han Chang'an City. In 3rd August, 2012, the Standing Committee of the CPC Xi'an Municipal Committee has approved the National Great Relics Protection Implementation Program of Han Chang'an City. Construction and administration bodies have been established. A relics protection program covering 36km² are now fully launched. The main structure construction and infrastructures such as water and road network will be completed within this year. The application for the world heritage of Weiyang Palace Heritage Site will be passed in June and the Front Hall Heritage Park of Weiyang Palace is expected to be open to the public in July.

秦岭北麓生态环境保护。秦岭北麓占西安国土面积的57.9%,是西安的生态屏障。目前,已完成大秦岭西安段《生态环境保护规划》和《保护利用总体规划》,正在实施重点峪口、重点景区的水电路等基础设施建设,今年上半年出台《西安市秦岭保护条例》,5月底前完成景观道路的雕塑、标识、设施,形成长安大道、子午大道和环山路景观长廊，力争一年出模样、两年出形象、三年大变样。

Eco-environmental Protection of the North Foot of Qinling Mountain. The North Foot of Qinling Mountain takes up 57.9% of the land area of Xi'an, serving as the green screen of the city. A series of projects such as Eco-environmental Protection Plan and Master Plan of Protection and Utilization of Qinling Mountain Xi'an Section have been set out. Infrastructures such as water and road network of major valley exits and scenic spots are now under construction. Conservation Regulation on Qinling Mountain will also be introduced on the first half of 2013. By the end of this May, constructions of the sculptures, signs and facilities along the main roads shall be finished. A Landscape corridor featuring Chang'an Avenue, Ziwu Avenue and Huanshan Road shall then be formed. Notable changes are expected to be taken place within 3 years.

八水润西安。2012年12月21日，市委常委会研究通过了《八水润西安规划》，加大对"5大引水源、7块湿地、10条河系、28个湖池"的改造提升，确保形成河连库、库连渠、渠连湖美景。今年重点是引汉济渭调节蓄水工程、

2平方公里昆明池（实验区）工程及灞河上游段河道治理等工程。

Eight Rivers Nourishing Xi'an. In 21st December, 2012, the Standing Committee of the CPC Xi'an Municipal Committee has approved the Project of Eight Rivers Nourishing Xi'an, stating that 5 major water sources, 7 wetlands, 10 river systems and 28 lakes and ponds shall be rebuilt and upgraded to form an interconnected water system. Key projects of 2013 includes Han River-to-Wei River Water Diversion, 2km² Kunming Pool Project and Management and Control Project of the Upper Bahe River.

公路交通枢纽建设。2012年11月31日，渭北大横线已开工。今年将开工建设西安北环线，规划东西312、310和南北210、108国道连接工程，对108国道、107省道进行扩能改造，使西安真正成为西部交通枢纽。

Road Transportation Hub Construction. Weibei Horizontal Line has commenced its construction in 31st Nov 2012. The construction of Xi'an North Ring Road will start this year. Linking project of National Highways 312, 310, 210 and 108, upgrade of National Highway 108, Provincial Highway 107 will also be launched. All the above-mentioned actions will enable Xi'an to become a real transportation hub of Western China.

农业经济
Agricultural Economy

农业生产
Agricultural Production

2012年主要农副产品产量
Output of Main Agricultural Products for 2012

农业产业化
Industrialization of Agriculture

西安概览
2013 A SURVEY OF XI'AN

农业生产

2012年,全市实现农林牧渔及服务业总产值308.36亿元,增长6.0%。全年粮食总产量192.54万吨,连续9年稳定在180万吨以上。

Agricultural Production

The Gross output of farming, forestry, animal husbandry and aquaculture took up 30.836 billion yuan in 2012, up by 6.0%. The grain output totaled 1.9254 million tons. The annual grain output remained stable at over 1.8 million ton for 9 consecutive years.

2012年主要农副产品产量

Output of Main Agricultural Products for 2012

产品名称 Product	计量单位 Unit	绝对值 Absolute Volume	比上年增长(%) Annual increase
粮食 Grain	万吨 10,000 tons	192.54	5.8
油料 Oil	万吨 10,000 tons	1.15	-1.7
蔬菜 Vegetable	万吨 10,000 tons	277.80	6.2
园林水果 Fruit	万吨 10,000 tons	93.21	2.3
肉类 Meat	万吨 10,000 tons	15.17	4.9
奶类 Dairy Products	万吨 10,000 tons	66.64	2.8
禽蛋 Egg	万吨 10,000 tons	13.00	3.4
水产品 Aquatic Products	万吨 10,000 tons	1.40	4.9
大牲畜年末存栏率 Livestock	万头 10,000	21.19	-0.2
猪年末存栏数 Pig	万头 10,000	96.60	2.3
羊年末存栏数 Sheep	万只 10,000	28.46	-3.9
家禽年末存栏数 Poultry	万只 10,000	1176.73	2.0

农业产业化

2012年，市级以上农业产业化重点龙头企业达到125家，其中，省级36家，国家级10家，完成销售收入210亿元；全市旅游观光农业总面积发展到35万亩，接待游客720万人次，经营收入11亿元。

Industrialization of Agriculture

In 2012, Xi'an has 125 leading agricultural industrialized enterprises of city-level and above, among which 36 are of provincial level and 10 are of national level, with total sales revenue of 21 billion yuan. Tourism sites in the rural area expanded to 350 thousand mu, receiving 7.2 million tourists and generating 1.1 billion yuan in revenue.

工业生产
Industrial Production

2012年主要工业产品产量
Output of Main Industrial Products for 2012

现代工业
Modern Industry

工业生产

2012年，全市规模以上工业完成总产值4023.19亿元，增长15.1%；规模以上工业实现增加值1144.29亿元，增长13.0%，实现利润132.80亿元。规模以上企业达到936户，其中陕重汽等6户企业产销超百亿元。

Industrial Production

In 2012, the above-scale industrial output reached 402.319 billion yuan, increased by 15.1%. The added value of above-scale industrial output counted up 114.429 billion yuan, up by 13.0%. The profit generated from industrial products reached 13.28 billion yuan. There are 936 above-scale industrial companies, 6 of which, including Shaanxi Heavy Truck Co, Ltd, achieved a sales volume amounting to over 10 billion yuan.

2012年主要工业产品产量

Output of Main Industrial Products for 2012

规模以上工业主要产品产量
Main Industrial Output produced by Above-scale enterprises

产品名称 Product	单位 Unit	产量 Output	比上年增长（%） Annual increase rate
发电量 Power Generating Capacity	亿千瓦小时 100millionKW/h	99.48	4.7
软饮料 Soft drinks	万吨 10,000 ton	204.05	0.0
小麦粉 Flour	万吨 10,000 ton	102.34	-5.1
机制纸 Machine-made paper and cardboard	万吨 10,000 ton	27.61	-31.1
汽油 Gasoline	万吨 10,000 ton	34.44	73.2
液化石油气 LPG	万吨 10,000 ton	6.71	48.7
配合饲料 Mixed feed stuff	万吨 10,000 ton	18.95	2.5
乳制品 Dairy products	万吨 10,000 ton	124.44	12.3
原油加工量 Crude oil processing volume	万吨 10,000 ton	217.47	42.0
钢材 Steel	万吨 10,000 ton	31.29	67.2
交流电动机 Alternate Current Motor	万千瓦 10,000 KW/h	442.79	-21.6
轿车 Car	万辆 10,000	36.62	-5.3
变压器 Transformer	万千伏安 10,000 KVA	10750.10	-5.9

第三产业
Tertiary Industry

金融保险
Finance and Insurance

零售商业
Retail Sales

交通运输
Transportation

城市公共交通
Urban Public Traffic

房地产业
Real Estate Industry

旅游业
Tourism Industry

会展业
Conventions and Exhibition

金融保险

2012年,全市共有各类银行业金融机构30家,其中外资银行机构3家。全部本外币存款余额和贷款余额分别达到12285.96亿元和8808.04亿元。全市共有各类保险公司48家(共有保险专业中介机构107家),全年保费收入176.78亿元,同比增长6.8%。

Finance and Insurance

In 2012, there are 30 financial institutions in Xi'an, 3 of which are foreign banks. Balance of deposits and loans (both domestic and foreign currency) amounted to 1228.596 billion yuan and 880.804 billion yuan respectively. Premium paid to 48 insurance companies (107 insurance institutions in total) counted up to 17.678 billion yuan, up by 6.8%.

零售商业

2012年,全市完成社会消费品零售总额2236.06亿元,同比增长15.5%。其中,汽车消费增长迅速,全年限额以上企业实现汽车销售34.48万辆、增长9.3%,实现汽车类零售额467.87亿元、增长6.4%。

Retail Sales

In 2012, retail sales volume of social consumption fulfilled 223.606 billion yuan, up by 15.5% compared with the same period of the previous year. In particular, auto consumption witnesses a strong boost. 344,800 autos were purchased in 2012 according to major auto sales companies, rose by 9.3%. Sales volume of vehicles reached 46.787 billion yuan, rose by 6.4%.

交通运输

2012年,铁路旅客发送量2918.70万人次,同比增长1.8%,货物发送量824.85万吨,同比增长0.2%;公路客运量3.09亿人次,同比增长5.2%,货运量44082万吨,同比增长14.8%;民航旅客吞吐量2342.09万人次,同比增长10.7%,货物吞吐量17.48万吨,同比增长1.3%。

Transportation

In 2012, the railway passenger transporting volume came to 29.187 million, a 1.8% increase, while the railway cargo transporting volume came to 8.2485 million tons, a 0.2% growth than that of last year. Highway passenger transporting volume hit 309million , up by 5.2% while the highway cargo transporting volume of the year hit 44.082 million tons, up by 14.8%.The civil airlines passenger handling capacity reached 23.4209 million ,increased by 10.7% and cargo handling capacity reached 174,800 ton, grew by 1.3%.

城市公共交通

城市公交快速、便捷，是市民出行的主要交通方式。至2012年末，全市共有公交线路243条，公交运营车辆7685台，全年完成客运量17.45亿人次。地铁建设取得新进展，地铁二号线于2011年9月16日通车运营，平均日客流量达到18万人次，突破了全国首条地铁线路开通初期客运量最高纪录。地铁一号线实现"电通轨通"，三号线全线和四号线试验段开工建设。

Urban Public Traffic

Urban public transport constitutes key means of transport for Xi'an citizens thanks to its speediness and convenience. By the end of 2012, there are 243 bus routes, with 7685 buses in operation, carrying 1.745 billion passengers in the whole year. Metro construction achieved new progress. Metro line 2 opened to the public on 16th September, 2011. The daily average passenger flow of Line 2 reached 180,000, higher than any initial passenger flow volume of the first subway in any other cities in China. All stations of Metro Line 1 have been capped. Line 3 and the experimental section of Line 4 have been put into construction.

房地产业

2012年,全市商品房销售面积1538.91万平方米。商品房施工面积9947.89万平方米,增长20.6%;竣工面积1063.70万平方米,增长68.6%。

Real Estate Industry

In 2012, sales volume of commercial housing reached 15.3891 million m^2. The area of the construction sites of commercial housing reached 99.4789 million m^2, up by 20.6%. 10.637 million m^2 housing has been completed, up by 68.6%.

旅游业

2012年,实现旅游业总收入654.39亿元,同比增长23.4%。接待国内游客7863万人次,增长20.0%;接待境外游客115.35万人次,增长15.1%。至2012年末,全市有星级宾馆121家,其中五星级宾馆9家,四星级27家;旅行社395家;A级景区(点)55个,其中5A景区3个、4A景区15个。

Tourism Industry

In 2012, total revenue generated from tourism amounted to 65.439 billion yuan, up by 23.4%. The number of domestic tourists reached 78.63 million while that of overseas tourists amounted to 1.1535 million, up by 20% and 15.1% respectively. By the end of 2012, there are 121 star-rated hotels (including 9 five-star hotels and 27 four-star hotels), 395 travel agencies and 55 grade A tourism attractions (including 3 grade 5A and 15 grade 4A) in Xi'an.

会展业

2012年，全市举办第十六届东西部合作与投资贸易洽谈会等规模展会160个，参展商25.6万人次，专业观众27.2万人次，新增就业岗位3.9万个，展会成交额1104亿元。

Convention and Exhibition

In 2012, Xi'an successfully held 160 conventions and exhibitions, including the 16th Investment and Trade Forum for Cooperation between East and West China. 256,000 exhibitors, 272,000 professional participators have taken part in the events. 39,000 new jobs are created. The transaction volume reached 110.4 billion yuan.

	参展国家（个）Participating Countries	参展商（名）participating businessmen	签订项目（个）Signed Contracts	合同金额（亿元）Contract Investment
第十六届西洽会 16th Investment and Trade Forum for Cooperation between East and West China	37	1594	377	3983.15

城市建设投资
Investment for Urban Construction

环境保护
Environment Protection

缓堵保畅
Relieving Traffic Congestion &
Ensuring Smooth Traffic Flow

城市精细化管理
Urban Delicacy Management

城市建设
Urban Construction

城市建设投资

2012年,全市完成城市维护建设投资246.8亿元,占全社会固定资产投资的比重为5.8%,建成区面积达到449平方公里,城市基础设施不断完善,城市综合承载力进一步提高。确立了主城区、3个副中心、5个组团和60个重点镇组成的城镇体系,逐步形成北跨渭河、南依秦岭、东联渭南、西接咸阳的城市空间布局。

Investment for Urban Construction

In 2012, investment on urban maintenance and construction reached 24.68 billion yuan, accounting for 5.8% of total fixed assets. Within the 449 km^2 main urban area, the infrastructure has been greatly improved, upgrading the city's overall handling capacity. Along with the relocation of the municipal administrative center, a new urban pattern of the combination of main downtown area, 3 sub-center, 5 clusters and 60 key towns has been formed, reaching Weihe River to the North, Qinling Mountain to the South, Weinan City to the East and Xianyang to the West.

近年来西安城市建设投资增长柱形图
See attached the graphic of Investment growth of
Urban Construction in Recent Years

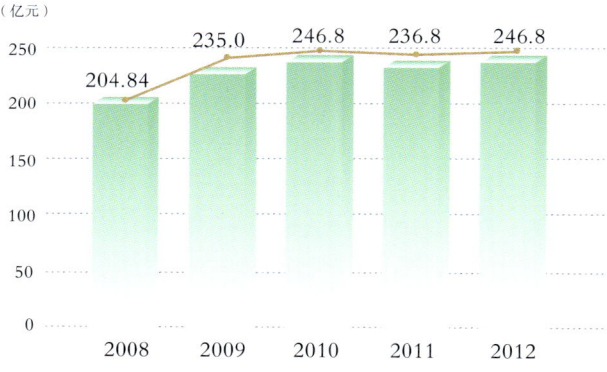

环境保护

2012年,全市空气质量好于国家二级标准(良好)以上天数306天;区域环境噪声等效声级均值为55.3分贝,道路交通噪声等效声级均值为68.2分贝,均达到国家相应标准。率先在西部城市实施PM2.5监测和发布。

Environment Protection

In 2012, 306 days in Xi'an met the State Grade II (Fine) ambiance air quality standard. The equivalent noise level of the local area averaged 55.3db, and that of the road transportation averaged 68.2db, both meeting the national standard. Xi'an takes the lead in Western China in monitoring and releasing the PM2.5 Index.

缓堵保畅

大力实施缓堵保畅工程,制定了缓堵保畅三年行动方案,明确43条具体措施,坚持反复抓、抓反复,连续抓3年。2012年,完成65处路段、交叉路口和64处公交港湾改造,建成43.8公

里公交专用道、8992个公共停车位,新城南客运站正式运营,"公交都市"试点工作有序推进。

Relieving Traffic Congestion & Ensuring Smooth Traffic Flow

The Project of Relieving Traffic Congestion & Ensuring Smooth Traffic Flow sets out the action plan in 3 years to solve the problems of urban traffic jam, highlights 43 specific countermeasures that need to be carried out and stressed in the next 3 years. Last year, 65 road sections, intersections, 65 bus stations have been reconstructed, 43.8km exclusive lane for public transportations and 8992 public parking spaces have been completed. The New South Passenger Terminal is officially put into operation. All works of building a Public Transport City are carrying forward smoothly.

城市精细化管理

召开城市精细化管理工作会议,确定今年为"城市精细化管理年",制定了《实施方案》,重点解决20类突出问题,大力提升规划、绿化、亮化、美化、细化水平,进一步彰显西安的历史人文、山水生态、古都风韵。去年,新栽大树2.74万棵,新增城市绿地面积445万平方米,完成造林面积5万亩,城市绿化覆盖率、森林覆盖率分别达到41.15%、44.99%。通过国家卫生城市复审。

Urban Delicacy Management

The year of 2013 has been defined as the Year of Urban Delicacy Management after the themed Working Conference. Implementation plan is made to tackle 20 types of major problems so as to improve the city's capacities of planning, afforestation, urban renewal, landscaping and delicacy, and therefore to further present the splendid history, profound culture, brilliant civilization and magnificent landscape of Xi'an. Last year, 27,400 trees are newly planted, 4.45 million m² green spaces are generated, 50,000 mu of afforestation are completed. The urban green coverage rate and forest coverage rate have been so far increased to 41.15% and 44.99% respectively. Xi'an has also passed the review for National Hygienic City.

招商引资
Attracting Foreign Investment

对外贸易
Foreign Trade

国际友好城市
International Sister-cities

对外开放
Opening to the Outside World

西安概览　2013 A SURVEY OF XI'AN

招商引资

2012年，批准外商直接投资合同项目87项，合同金额36.03亿美元，实际利用金额24.78亿美元，增长23.6%。全市在建内资项目623个，实际到位资金1201.2亿元，其中新建项目438个，合同引资额3900.72亿元，实际到位资金692.7亿元。

Attracting Foreign Investment

In 2012, 87 foreign direct investment projects were approved, contracting 3.603 billion USD. The actual use of foreign capital reached 2.478 billion USD, increased by 23.6%. 623 inward investment projects are currently under construction, with fully funded investment amount as much as 120.12 billion yuan. 438 of the projects are newly started, with contract investment amount as much as 390.072 billion yuan, fully funded of 69.27 billion yuan.

对外贸易

2012年，西安地区对外贸易总值130.14亿美元，其中自营进出口总值118.02亿美元，增长4.6%。服务外包合同金额5.45亿美元，增长40.5%。

Foreign Trade

In 2012, foreign trade volume in Xi'an valued 13.014 billion USD, within which the self-supporting import and export volume totaled 9.986 billion USD, increased by 29.8%. Business outsourcing offshore export volume added up to 545 million USD, increased by 40.5%.

国际友好城市

至2012年末，西安已与19个国家的21个城市结为友好城市。

International Sister-cities

By the end of 2012, Xi'an has established sister-city relationship with 21 cities from 19 nations.

与西安市结为友好城市的国际城市及缔结时间

A List of Sister Cities and Time of Establishing the Relationship

日本 Japan	奈良市	Nara	1974年2月1日 Feb. 1, 1974
日本 Japan	京都市	Kyoto	1974年5月10日 May 10, 1974
英国 U.K.	爱丁堡市	Edinburgh	1985年4月16日 Apr. 16, 1985
法国 France	波城市	Pau	1986年9月15日 Sep. 15, 1986
美国 U.S.A.	堪萨斯市	Kansas	1989年4月29日 Apr. 29, 1989
伊朗 Iran	伊斯法罕市	Esfahan	1989年5月6日 May 6, 1989
德国 Germany	多特蒙德市	Dortmund	1991年5月27日 May 27, 1991
巴基斯坦 Pakistan	拉合尔市	Lahore	1992年6月20日 Jun. 20, 1992
日本 Japan	船桥市	Funabashi	1994年11月2日 Nov. 2, 1994
韩国 South Korea	庆州市	Kyongju	1994年11月18日 Nov. 18, 1994
罗马尼亚 Romania	雅西市	Lasi	1994年12月6日 Dec. 6, 1994
乌克兰 Ukraine	第聂伯罗彼得罗夫斯克市	Dnepropetrovsk	1995年10月27日 Oct. 27, 1995
土耳其 Turkey	科尼亚市	Konya	1996年9月8日 Sep. 8, 1996
尼泊尔 Nepal	加德满都市	Kathmandu	1996年9月12日 Sep. 12, 1996
巴西 Brazil	巴西利亚市	Brasilia	1997年10月26日 Oct. 26, 1997
加拿大 Canada	魁北克市	Quebec	2001年5月11日 May 11, 2001
阿根廷 Argentina	科尔多瓦市	Cordoba	2006年12月19日 Dec. 19, 2006
意大利 Italy	庞贝市	Pompeii	2007年10月13日 Oct. 13, 2007
希腊 Greece	卡拉马塔市	Kalamata	2009年9月17日 Sep. 19, 2009
厄瓜多尔 Ecuador	昆卡市	Cuenca	2010年9月8日 Sep. 8, 2010
荷兰 The Netherlands	格罗宁根市	Groningen	2011年11月7日 Nov. 7, 2011

居民收入
Resident Income

居民消费
Resident Consumption

居住条件
Resident Housing Condition

社会保障
Social Security

人民生活
People's livelihood

居民收入

2012年,西安市城镇居民人均可支配收入29982元,增长15.4%;农村居民人均纯收入11442元,增长16.9%。

Resident Income

In 2012, the per capita disposable income of urban residents reached 29,982 yuan, increased by 15.4%. The net income of rural residents reached 11,442 yuan, grew by 16.9%.

居民消费

2012年,西安市城镇居民家庭人均消费性支出21434元,增长11.0%。农村居民家庭人均生活消费支出7774元,增长15.9%。

Resident Consumption

In 2012, per capita expenditure in urban household was 21,434 yuan, up by 11.0%. Per capita expenditure in rural household was 7,774 yuan, up by 15.9%.

居住条件

全年住宅新开工面积2313.67万平方米,增长7.9%,其中经济适用房开工建设335.78万平方米,竣工52.78万平方米。廉租房住房保障户数累计达到28549户,实现制度性

全覆盖。2012年末,全市城镇居民人均住房建筑面积32.98平方米,农村居民人均住房面积78平方米。

Resident Housing Condition

23.1367 million m² of houses were newly-built, up by 7.9%. Among them, 3.3578 million m² are affordable housing for low-income residents, with 527, 800 m² having been completed. 28,549 families living in poverty are covered by low-rent housing. By the end of 2012, per capita housing area for urban residents reached 32.98 m² while that for rural residents reached 78 m².

社会保障
Social Security

类 别 Category	绝对值(万人) Absolute Volume 10,000 person	新增(万人) Increased Volume 10,000 person
基本养老保险 Pension insurance	241.63	25.83
基本医疗保险 Medical Insurance	413.60	9.33
失业保险 Unemployment insurance	139.84	5.02
工伤保险 Injury Insurance	133.47	10.40
生育保险 Maternity Insurance	97.19	1.74
最低生活保障 Minimum living security	29.4	-2.6
新农合 Rural medical insurance	397.53	2.68

科技教育
Science, Technology and Education

科研力量
Scientific Research Strength

科技投入
Investment on science and technology

科技成果
Science and Technological Achievements

高等教育
Higher Education

普通教育
General Education

民办教育
Private Education

成人教育
Adult Education

2012年各级各类学校情况
Information for Different Categories of Schools

西安概览 2013 A SURVEY OF XI'AN

科研力量

西安科技力量雄厚、人才众多。至2012年末，拥有各类科研及开发机构3000多个，各类独立科研机构460余家，其中国家级重点实验室、工程技术研究中心和行业测试中心231个，各类专业技术人员44万人，两院院士55人。

Scientific Research Strength

Xi'an is strong in science and technology and has a large number of highly-skilled talents. By the end of 2012, it has over 3,000 R&D institutions and 460 independent scientific research institutions, including 231 national key labs and engineering testing centers staffed by 440,000 professionals and 55academicians from Chinese Academy of Sciences and Chinese Academy of Engineering.

科技投入

2012年，全市财政科技投入达5.93亿元，较上年增加0.71亿元，增长13.6%，占全市一般预算财政支出1%。

Investment on science and technology

In 2012, 593 million yuan have been invested in science and technology, 71 million yuan more than that of last year, increased by 13.6%, accounting for 1% of the general budget expenditure of Xi'an.

科技成果

2012年，全市实现技术市场交易额300.22亿元，居副省级城市第1位。专利申请量36983件，连续八年保持

30%以上的增幅,其中发明专利申请量为15029件,同比增长28.75%,居副省级城市第3位。每万人发明专利拥有量达到11.28件,是全国平均值的3.5倍。

Science and Technological Achievements

In 2012, the trading volume in technology market reached 30.022 billion yuan, ranking the first among all sub-provincial cities. The patent application was 36,983, increased by 30% and above for 8 consecutive years, among which there are 15,029 inventive patents, increased by 28.75%, ranking the 3rd among sub-provincial cities. Patent density reached 11.28 (per 10,000 person), 3.5 times higher than the national average.

高等教育

至2012年末,全市共有研究生培养单位46家,全年研究生教育共招生2.81万人,毕业生2.30万人。全市普通高等院校62所,全年共招收本科、专科学生22.46万人,在校学生72.40万人。

Higher Education

By the end of 2012, 46 higher education institutions with postgraduate qualification have recruited 28,100 postgraduate students and have brought about 23,000 graduates. There are 62 colleges and universities in Xi'an, recruiting 224,600 undergraduate and junior college students, with a total on-campus student number as large as 724,000.

普通教育

2012年,全市共有小学1322所,普通中学419所,中等专业学校30所。全市九年义务教育入学率99.87％。

General Education

In 2012, there are 1,322 primary schools, 419 middle schools and 30 secondary vocational schools in Xi'an. Nine-year compulsory school enrollment rate reached 99.87%.

民办教育

2012年,全市共有民办高校(机构)25所(个),在校学生23.73万人。民办普通中学50所,在校学生7.52万人;民办小学36所,在校学生4.64万人;民办幼儿园990所,在校学生18.99万人。

Private Education

In 2012, Xi'an has 25 private higher education institutions with 237,300 on-campus students, 50 Private middle schools with 75,200 students, 36 private primary schools with 46,400 students and 990 private kindergartens with 189,900 kids.

成人教育

2012年，全市共有成人高校15所，在校学生15.98万人；成人技术培训学校2048所，培训结业学员47.69万人，有54.38万人参加学习及接受培训，教职工0.99万人。

Adult Education

In 2012, Xi'an has 15 adult colleges with 159,800 on-campus students. 476,900 students in Xi'an have completed the training courses offered by 2048 vocational schools. 543,800 people have taken the training courses. The number of school faculties reached 9,900.

2012年各级各类学校情况

Information for Different Categories of Schools

类别 Category	学校(所) Number of Schools	专任教师(万人) Number of Full-time Teachers(10,000)	在校学生(万人) Number of Students (10,000)
普通高等教育 Regular higher education	62	4.01	96.85
成人高等教育 Adult higher education	15	0.15	15.98
中学 Middle Schools	419	3.15	45.33
中等职业教育学校 Secondary Vocational Schools	108	0.58	13.42
小学 Primary Schools	1322	2.97	50.85
特殊教育学校 Special Schools	8	0.025	0.14

卫生事业
Public Health and Medical Care

文化事业
Cutural Undertakings

新闻出版
Press and Publication

体育事业
Sports Activities

社会事业
Social Undertakings

卫生事业

2012年,全市拥有各类医疗卫生机构5576个,其中,医院、卫生院376个,疾病预防控制中心17所;拥有各类卫生技术人员6.64万人,其中执业(助理)医师2.31万人;拥有医院病床4.42万张。社区卫生服务网络覆盖城区。全市建立社区卫生服务中心128所、社区卫生服务站73个。

Public Health and Medical Care

In 2012, there are 5,576 medical institutions of all levels in Xi'an, including 376 hospitals and 17 disease prevention & control centers. Among the 66,400 medical staff, 23,100 are licensed (assistant) doctors. The number of ward beds totaled 44,200 There are 128 community health service centers and 73 community health service stations, covering all urban area.

文化事业

2012年,全市有艺术团体13个,公共图书馆15个,博物馆94座,电视台1座,广播电台1座,广播电视台7座。电视人口覆盖率98.83%,广播人口覆盖率99.45%。

Cultural Undertakings

In 2012, there are 13 art performance groups, 15 public libraries, 94 museums, 1 TV stations, 1 broadcasting stations and 7 broadcasting TV stations in Xi'an. The audience coverage of TV reached 98.83% and that of broadcasting was up to 99.45%.

新闻出版

2012年,全年共出版报纸43种,杂志224种,图书6630种,音像186种。

Press and Publication

Various kinds of publications including 43 newspapers, 224 magazines, 6,630 books and 186 audiovisual products are issued in 2012.

体育事业

全市拥有各类体育场馆4827个,全市体育人口达到42%,位于全国前列。农民体育健身工程1616个,拥有社会体育指导员8600名。在2012年伦敦奥运会上,我市运动员获得了两金一银的好成绩。

Sports Activities

4,827 sport fields and venues are available in Xi'an. 42% of the citizens do exercises regularly, ranking high in China. 1616 sports projects catering for farmers were worked out. 8,600 coaches give sports guidance in communities. Athletes from Xi'an have won 2 gold and 1 silver medals in London Olympics 2012.

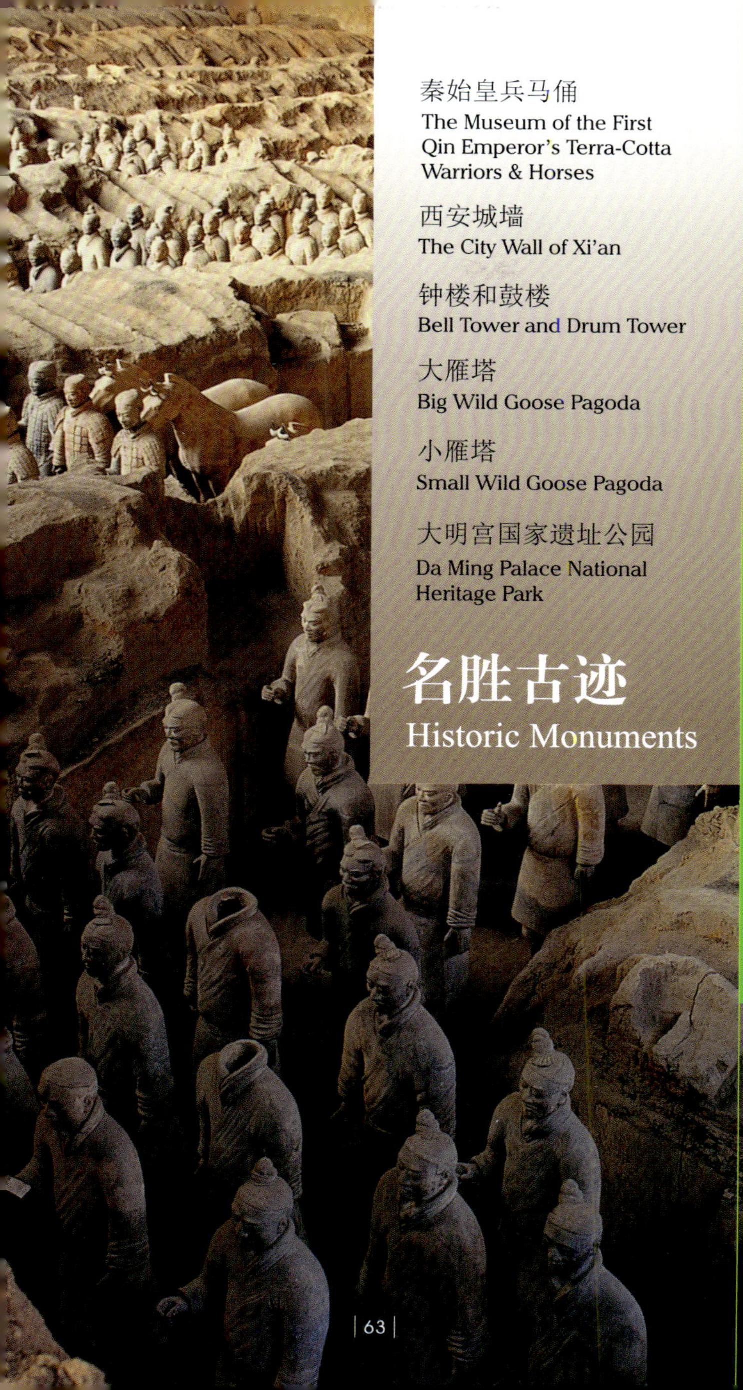

秦始皇兵马俑
The Museum of the First Qin Emperor's Terra-Cotta Warriors & Horses

西安城墙
The City Wall of Xi'an

钟楼和鼓楼
Bell Tower and Drum Tower

大雁塔
Big Wild Goose Pagoda

小雁塔
Small Wild Goose Pagoda

大明宫国家遗址公园
Da Ming Palace National Heritage Park

名胜古迹
Historic Monuments

西安概览

2013 A SURVEY OF XI'AN

西安的文化遗存具有资源密度大、保存好、级别高的特点，在我国旅游资源普查的155个基本类型中，西安旅游资源占据89个。西安周围帝王陵墓有72座，其中有"千古一帝"秦始皇的陵墓，周、秦、汉、唐四大都城遗址，西汉帝王11陵和唐代帝王18陵，大小雁塔、钟鼓楼、古城墙等古建筑700多处。

Cultural heritage in Xi'an is densely-distributed, well-preserved and highly-valued. Out of the 155 basic types of tourism resources in light of the national survey, 89 are in Xi'an. 72 imperial mausoleums are scattered in and around Xi'an, represented by the Qin Mausoleum of the "First Emperor in One-thousand-year History". Some 700 monuments could be found in Xi'an, such as capital ruins of Zhou, Qin, Han and Tang Dynasties, 11 mausoleums of West Han emperors and 18 mausoleums of Tang emperors, the Big and Small Wild Goose Pagodas, the Bell Tower, the Drum Tower and the ancient City Wall.

秦始皇兵马俑

秦始皇兵马俑位于西安临潼区，兵马俑坑规模宏大，占地约2万多平方米，被誉为"世界第八大奇迹"。坑内共有陶俑马近八千件，木制战车一百余乘，青铜兵器4万余件。1987年由联合国教科文组织列入"世界人类文化遗产"目录，被评为国家5A级旅游景区。

The Museum of the First Qin Emperor's Terra-Cotta Warriors & Horses

The overwhelming Museum of Emperor Qin Shihuang's TThe overwhelming Museum of Emperor Qin Shihuang's Terra-Cotta Warriors & Horses has won the reputation of "The 8th Wonder in the World". Situated in Lintong district of Xi'an, the museum covers an area of over 20,000 m^2. There are 8,000 pieces of terra-cotta warriors and horses, more than 100 wooden chariots and 40,000 bronze weapons in the pits. In 1987, it was listed as World Cultural Heritage site by UNESCO. It was also appraised as National 5A Grade tourism attraction.

西安城墙

西安城墙始建于明洪武三年至十一年（公元1370年至1378年），是目前我国乃至世界上规模最大，保存最完整的古城垣建筑，1961年被国务院公布为第一批全国重点文物保护单位。

西安城墙为东西向长方形，用夯土板筑而成，周长13.75公里，城垣高（包括垛墙）12米，城内面积约12平方公里。绕城一周约14公里（中心线距）。护城河宽14-24米，各门闸楼下设可起落吊桥一座，共4座，现只恢复南门一座。

The City Wall of Xi'an

Xi'an City Wall, built from 1370 to 1378 during the reign of Hongwu in Ming Dynasty, represents the largest, best-preserved Chinese wall-circled construction. In 1961, the State Council announced it key cultural heritage under state protection.

Xi'an City Wall takes a rectangular shape. Being built of rammed earth, it is 13.75 km in length, 12 meters in height and covers an area of 12 km^2. A 14 to 24- meter-wide moat runs 14 km around the City Wall. At the 4 main gates, there used to be 4 suspension bridges which could be lifted and lowered. Now only the one at the South Gate was renovated.

钟楼和鼓楼

钟楼，始建于明太祖朱元璋洪武十七年（公元1384年），因楼上悬挂铁钟而得名。钟楼为砖木结构，从下至上依次由基座、楼体及宝顶三部分组成，总高36米，是我国古代留存下来众多钟楼中形制最大、保存最完整的一座。

鼓楼，始建于明太祖朱元璋洪武十三年（公元1380年）。楼上原有巨鼓一面，每日击鼓报时，故称"鼓楼"。鼓楼总高34米，其建筑形式是歇山式重檐三滴水，是目前全国现存最大的鼓楼。

Bell Tower and Drum Tower

Bell Tower was built in 1384, the 17th year during the reign of Emperor Zhu Yuanzhang of Ming dynasty. The tower gained the name from an iron bell hung in it. The 36-meter-high, brick –and –wood tower is made up of base, main tower and roof. It proved to be the largest, best-preserved bell tower that survived the long Chinese History.

Drum Tower was built in 1380, the 13th year during the reign of Emperor Zhu Yuanzhang of Ming dynasty. There used to be a huge drum in the tower which struck time at dusk, hence the name Drum Tower. The 34-meter-high Drum Tower is the largest of its kind in China. The building is a Xieshan-style, multi-tier eaves structure.

大雁塔

　　大雁塔,是唐高宗永徽三年(公元652年),唐三藏法师玄奘为保存从印度带回的经典和佛像,在大慈恩寺内建造的藏经塔。大雁塔是中国楼阁式砖塔的优秀代表作,塔分7层,通高64米,底边各长25米,通体呈方形角锥状。沿塔内木梯盘旋而上,可达塔顶。

Big Wild Goose Pagoda

　　Big Wild Goose Pagoda was built in 652, the third year during the reign of Emperor Yonghui of Tang dynasty. Monk Xuanzang, a prominent Buddhist scholar, built the pagoda in order to store the scriptures and statues brought back from India. The 7-story, 64-meter-high, 25-meter-wide pagoda represents the high achievement of Chinese brick tower architecture. The wooden stairs twist up to the top.

小雁塔

小雁塔，是唐景龙元年（公元707年），唐中宗李显在荐福寺南边安仁坊建造的一座秀丽的15层砖塔，其形状像大雁塔，塔身比大雁塔小，因此叫"小雁塔"。小雁塔现余13层，高43米，塔基呈正方形，底边各长11.38米。此塔基底小而重心高，因此历经70多次地震、1000多年风雨而仅顶部残破，塔身多次裂缝而不倒。

Small Wild Goose Pagoda

Small Wild Goose Pagoda was built by Tang dynasty Emperor Lixian in 707. It used to be a 15-story delicate brick tower situated to the south of Jianfu Temple. The pagoda gained the present name because it was in the shape of Big Wild Goose Pagoda in smaller size. The 43-meter-high, 11.38-meter-wide, rectangular-shaped Small Wild Goose Pagoda survived 70 earthquakes over 1,000 years and stood firmly in spite of the crack and the broken top.

大明宫国家遗址公园

大明宫遗址是我国目前保存最完整的皇宫遗址，是第一批全国重点文物保护单位，已作为丝绸之路跨国申报世界遗产的重点项目列入中国世界文化遗产预备名单。大明宫国家遗址公园，于2010年10月1日建成开园，以"保护文物、传承文明、弘扬文化、改善民生、提升城市"为建设宗旨，是西安市科学保护古迹遗址与城市发展和谐共生的最新实践成果。

Da Ming Palace National Heritage Park

Da Ming Palace National Heritage Park, opened to public on October 1, 2010, is the best-preserved imperial historical remains in China. It is one of the key items on the list of the trans-national Silk Road World Heritage project, which is expected to be approved by UNESCO. Adhering to the principal of "Preserving Cultural Heritage, Inheriting Civilization, Spreading Culture, Improving People's Living Condition and Upgrading City", the Da Ming Palace National Heritage Park is the best demonstration project showcasing the harmonious coordination between protection and development.

开发区建设

Construction of Development Zones

国家级西安高新技术产业开发区
The National Xi'an Hi-tech Industries Development Zone (XHTZ)

国家级西安经济技术开发区
The National Xi'an Economic & Technological Development Zone (XETDZ)

西安曲江新区
Xi'an Qujiang New District

西安浐灞生态区
Xi'an Chanba Ecological District

西安阎良国家航空高技术产业基地
Xi'an Yanliang National Aviation Hi-Tech Industrial Base (CABI)

西安国家民用航天产业基地
Xi'an National Civil Aerospace Industrial Base

西安国际港务区
Xi'an international Trade and Logistics Zone

西安沣东新城
Xi'an Fengdong New Town

西安概览

2013 A SURVEY OF XI'AN

国家级西安高新技术产业开发区

西安高新技术开发区是1991年3月经国务院首批批准设立的国家级高新技术产业开发区。2002年12月，被联合国工业发展组织考察认定为六个"中国最具活力的城市和地区"之一，是国家ISO14000示范区、国家标准示范园、国家知识产权试点园区和海外高层次人才创新创业基地。2005年6月17日，国家确定西安高新区在内的六个高新区建成世界一流的高技术园区。

The National Xi'an Hi-tech Industries Development Zone (XHTZ)

Founded in March 1991, XHTZ was among the first batch of the National Hi-tech Industries Development Zones approved by the State Council. It has been recognized by United Nations Industrial Development Organization as one of the six "Most Vigorous Cities and Regions in China" in December, 2002. XHTZ is crowned with the titles of national ISO14000 zone, national standard demonstration zone, national intellectual property right pilot zone and base for overseas talent to start up business. In 17th Jun, 2005, the National Government instructed that 6 hi-tech zones including XHTZ would be built into world-class hi-tech parks.

国家级西安经济技术开发区

西安经济技术开发区成立于1993年，2000年被国务院批准为国家级经济技术开发区，2002年设立国家级陕西西安出口加工区，2006年成为全国首批开展保税物流功能试点的国家级出口加工区，2010年被工信部批准为首批国家新型工业化产业示范基地。目前，开发区已初步成为一个外向型的现代化工业园区和城市新区。

The National Xi'an Economic & Technological Development Zone (XETDZ)

Established in 1993, XETDZ has been approved by the State Council in2000 as National Development Zone. The Export Processing Zone at the national level was established in 2002. In 2006 XETDZ has become one of the first national export processing zones with bonded logistic functions and has been approved by the Ministry of Industry and Information Technology as one of the first New Industrialization Demonstration Bases. Upon till now, XETDZ has evolved to be an export-oriented modernized industrial park and a new urban district .

西安曲江新区

西安曲江新区，2007年8月被国家文化部授予首个国家级文化产业示范区，是中西部地区首批国家级生态区，是以盛唐文化为特色、文化旅游产业为主导，集休闲、商贸为一体的城市新区。

Xi'an Qujiang New District

With culture and tourism as the mainstay industry, the district integrates the functions of recreation, entertainment and commerce. On August, 2007, Qujiang New District was awarded the first state-level cultural demonstration zone by the Ministry of Culture.

西安浐灞生态区

西安浐灞生态区成立于2004年9月，是中西部地区首批国家级生态区，是以"都市型生态区、生态化商务地"为发展定位的西安第三代新城，这里有国家级生态湿地公园和欧亚经济论坛永久会址。2011世界园艺博览会在此举办。

Xi'an Chanba Ecological District

Established on September, 2004, Chanba Ecological District is the first ecological district of national level in Midwest China. It is also a third- generation district featured as ecological zone in urban area and business destination with ecological characteristic. It is home to National Wetland Park, the permanent venue of Euro-Asia Economic Forum and the site of Xi'an International Horticultural Exposition 2011.

西安阎良国家航空高技术产业基地

西安阎良国家航空高技术产业基地设立于2004年8月，是国家发改委批准的我国唯一集航空产业研发、航空人才培养、航空装备生产及整机制造、零部件加工、航空服务为一体的国家级航空高技术产业基地。2010年6月，经国务院批准，该基地升级为国家级陕西航空经济技术开发区，跻身国家级开发区行列。

Xi'an Yanliang National Aviation Hi-Tech Industrial Base (CAIB)

Established by the State on August, 2004, CAIB is the only aviation hi-tech industrial base that integrates aviation industrial research, aviation talents cultivation, manufacturing of aviation equipment and aircrafts, processing of aircraft components as well as supporting services. In June, 2010, it was authorized to be a state-level aviation base by the State Council.

西安国家民用航天产业基地

西安国家民用航天产业基地成立于2006年11月，基地围绕航天运载动力和航天技术应用产业，重点发展信息技术、航天新材料、航天特种技术应用等。2010年6月，经国务院批准，该基地升级为国家级陕西航天经济技术开发区。

Xi'an National Civil Aerospace Industrial Base

Established on November, 2006, Xi'an Aerospace Scientific and Technological Base focuses on the application of aerospace technology, information technology and special material in aerospace sector. In June, 2010, it was authorized to be a state-level Aerospace Base by the State Council.

西安国际港务区

西安国际港务区成立于2008年4月，是国务院批准的西北首个综合保税区，获评2010年中国十佳物流园区。国际港务区是以现代商贸物流产业为突出特色的国际化、生态化、信息化、现代化的省级

开发区，力争发展成为全国最大的国际性陆港、黄河中上游地区最大的物流中心和商贸集散中心。

Xi'an international Trade and Logistics Zone

Established in April, 2008, the state-level International Trade and Logistics Zone was awarded 2010 top ten Chinese logistics zone. It was the first bonded zone in the northwest region of China. As a provincial-level development zone featuring modern trade and logistics, ecology and information, the zone is determined to be built into the largest international inland port in China and the largest distribution center in middle and upper reaches of the Yellow River.

西安沣东新城

西安沣东新城成立于2010年2月，位于渭河以南、西宝公路以北、东接西三环、西接沣河，规划面积159.3平方公里，是西咸新区的重要组成部分，是打造全国内陆型经济开放开发战略高地的重要承载区，也是西安国际化大都市建设的重要城市功能新区。

Xi'an Fengdong New Town

Covering a planned area of 159.3 km^2, Fengdong New Town, which was established on February, 2010, is situated to the south of Weihe River and to the north of Xibao highway, adjacent to the West 3rd Ring Road and Fenghe River. It is an important component of Xixian New Area, shouldering the strategic responsibility of accelerating the inland economy as well as building Xi'an into an international metropolis.

区县概况
Districts and Counties

未央区
Weiyang District

新城区
Xincheng District

莲湖区
Lianhu District

周至县
Zhouzhi County

户县
Huxian County

西安市区县区域地图
Map of Xi'an Districts and Counties

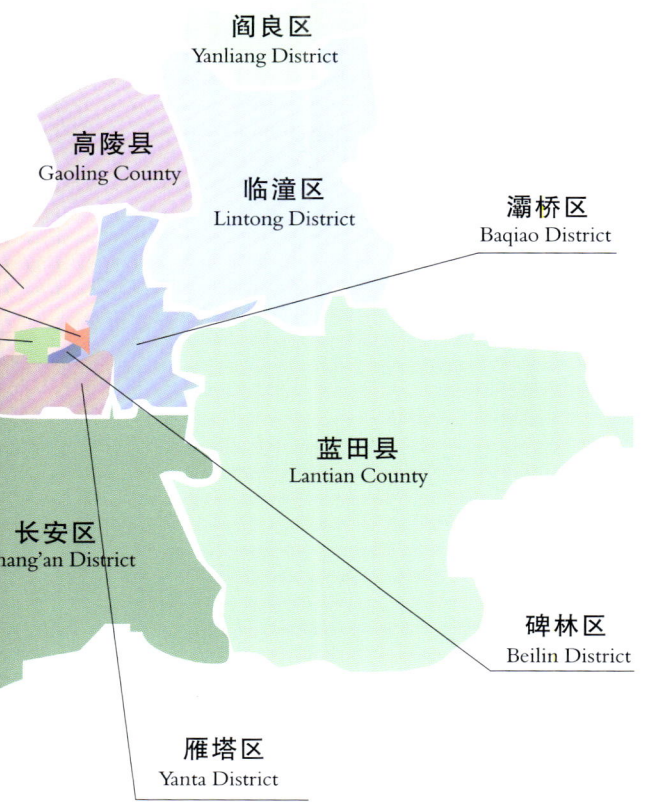

"五区一港两基地"主要经济指标
Main Economic Index for 8 Development Zones

名称 Name	规模以上工业增加值 Added Value for Above-Scale Industries		全社会固定资产投资 Investment for Fixed Assets	
	2012年（亿元） 2012 (100million Yuan)	比上年增长(%) Annual increase (%)	2012年（亿元） 2012 (100million Yuan)	比上年增长(%) Annual increase (%)
高新技术产业开发区 The National Xi'an Hi-tech Industries Development Zone (XHTZ)	185.20	17.2	418.44	25.1
经济技术开发区 The National Xi'an Economic & Technological Development Zone (XETDZ)	239.36	17.5	381.24	27.2
曲江新区 Qujiang New District	−	−	356.10	32.8
浐灞生态区 Chanhe & Bahe Rivers Ecological District	−	−	150.67	50.5
航空高技术产业基地 Yanliang National Aviation Hi-Tech Industrial Base (CABI)	2.97	35.5	48.39	35.9
民用航天产业基地 Xi'an National Civil Aerospace Industrial Base	22.23	20.3	62.94	36.3
国际港务区 Xi'an International Trade and Logistics Zone	−	−	58.16	65.1
沣东新城 Fengdong New Town	29.46	3.8	77.72	38.0

名称 Name	地方财政一般预算收入 Local Fiscal Revenue		实际利用外商直接投资 FDI in Actual Use	
	2012年（亿元） 2012 (100million Yuan)	比上年增长(%) Annual increase (%)	2012年（万美元） 2012 (10,000 dollars)	比上年增长(%) Annual increase (%)
高新技术产业开发区 The National Xi'an Hi-tech Industries Development Zone (XHTZ)	57.75	25.6	81776	25.9
经济技术开发区 The National Xi'an Economic & Technological Development Zone (XETDZ)	23.91	32.7	68202	25.8
曲江新区 Qujiang New District	21.12	47.4	26433	25.9
浐灞生态区 Chanhe & Bahe Rivers Ecological District	8.20	26.1	4837	25.4
航空高技术产业基地 Yanliang National Aviation Hi-Tech Industrial Base (CABI)	0.45	43.0	2072	21.8
民用航天产业基地 Xi'an National Civil Aerospace Industrial Base	2.26	32.9	2403	18.4
国际港务区 Xi'an International Trade and Logistics Zone	0.86	66.3	2082	32.5
沣东新城 Fengdong New Town	1.34	52.7	1876	25.0

2012年全市各区县经济社会主要指标
Main Economic and Social Index for Xi'an Districts and Counties in 2012

名称 Name	土地面积 Land Acreage		常住人口 Permanent Resident Population		城镇化率（%） Urbanization Rate (%)
	平方公里 km²	占全市比重（%） Proportion of the whole city values (%)	万人 10,000 People	占全市比重（%） Proportion of the whole city values (%)	
西安市 Xi'an	10108	–	855.29	–	71.51
新城区 Xincheng District	30	0.3	59.44	6.9	100.00
碑林区 Beilin District	24	0.2	62.08	7.3	100.00
莲湖区 Lianhu District	43	0.4	70.25	8.2	100.00
灞桥区 Baqiao District	325	3.2	60.16	7.0	92.54
未央区 Weiyang District	262	2.6	81.46	9.5	91.15
雁塔区 Yanta District	149	1.5	118.89	13.9	100.00
阎良区 Yanliang District	244	2.4	28.23	3.3	55.22
临潼区 Lintong District	915	9.1	66.45	7.8	31.98
长安区 Chang'an District	1590	15.7	109.54	12.8	55.69
蓝田县 Lantian County	2008	19.9	51.88	6.1	27.14
周至县 Zhouzhi County	2949	29.2	57.00	6.7	28.89
户　县 Huxian County	1282	12.7	56.10	6.6	39.00
高陵县 Gaoling County	287	2.8	33.81	4.0	61.43

2012年全市各区县经济社会主要指标（续1）
Main Economic and Social Index for Xi'an Districts and Counties in 2012 (Continue Ⅰ)

名 称 Name	地区生产总值 Regional GDP			规模以上工业增加值 Added Value for Above-Scale Industries		
	绝对额 （亿元） Absolute Value (100 million yuan)	增长 （%） Increase Rate (%)	占全市比重 （%） Proportion of the whole city values (%)	绝对额 （亿元） Absolute Value (100 million yuan)	增长 （%） Increase Rate (%)	占全市比重 （%） Proportion of the whole city values (%)
西安市 Xi'an	4369.37	11.8	–	1144.29	13.0	–
新城区 Xincheng District	430.22	11.5	9.8	96.46	10.2	8.4
碑林区 Beilin District	504.28	13.2	11.5	45.65	10.1	4.0
莲湖区 Lianhu District	479.40	11.5	11.0	130.50	8.9	11.4
灞桥区 Baqiao District	233.30	13.8	5.3	91.77	14.5	8.0
未央区 Weiyang District	516.73	9.5	11.8	164.34	9.1	14.4
雁塔区 Yanta District	810.83	11.4	18.6	127.87	15.6	11.2
阎良区 Yanliang District	141.49	12.2	3.2	53.82	15.0	4.7
临潼区 Lintong District	211.53	12.2	4.8	100.21	14.1	8.8
长安区 Chang'an District	362.64	13.2	8.3	118.36	14.2	10.3
蓝田县 Lantian County	95.73	11.0	2.2	13.29	11.1	1.2
周至县 Zhouzhi County	78.28	11.0	1.8	6.16	18.2	0.5
户 县 Huxian County	142.13	9.5	3.3	34.59	8.5	3.0
高陵县 Gaoling County	228.16	18.0	5.2	161.27	19.5	14.1

2012年全市各区县经济社会主要指标（续2）
Main Economic and Social Index for Xi'an Districts and Counties in 2012（Continue Ⅱ）

名 称 Name	全社会固定资产投资 Investment for Fixed Assets			社会消费品零售总额 Retail Sales Volume for Social Consumption		
	绝对额 （亿元） Absolute Value (100 million yuan)	增长 （%） Increase Rate (%)	占全市比重 （%） Proportion of the whole city values (%)	绝对额 （亿元） Absolute Value (100 million yuan)	增长 （%） Increase Rate (%)	占全市比重 （%） Proportion of the whole city values (%)
西安市 Xi'an	4243.43	26.6	–	2236.06	15.5	–
新城区 Xincheng District	353.50	24.1	8.3	387.86	15.4	17.3
碑林区 Beilin District	376.45	24.4	8.9	389.81	15.1	17.4
莲湖区 Lianhu District	473.49	25.3	11.2	322.70	15.2	14.4
灞桥区 Baqiao District	236.36	31.9	5.6	54.81	19.0	2.5
未央区 Weiyang District	568.99	26.9	13.4	318.47	14.6	14.2
雁塔区 Yanta District	956.06	23.0	22.5	425.72	16.1	19.0
阎良区 Yanliang District	154.52	27.8	3.6	26.58	15.8	1.2
临潼区 Lintong District	152.20	29.1	3.6	54.93	15.6	2.5
长安区 Chang'an District	406.99	30.5	9.6	125.86	16.7	5.6
蓝田县 Lantian County	99.54	29.7	2.3	40.49	15.7	1.8
周至县 Zhouzhi County	89.14	30.2	2.1	26.99	16.3	1.2
户 县 Huxian County	140.33	29.0	3.3	44.37	15.5	2.0
高陵县 Gaoling County	235.87	32.8	5.6	17.47	18.0	0.8

2012年全市各区县经济社会主要指标（续3）
Main Economic and Social Index for Xi'an Districts and Counties in 2012 (Continue III)

名 称 Name	地方财政一般预算收入 Local Fiscal Revenue			实际利用外商直接投资 FDI in Actual Use		
	绝对额 （亿元） Absolute Value (100 million yuan)	增长 （%） Increase Rate (%)	占全市比重 （%） Proportion of the whole city values (%)	绝对额 （万美元） Absolute Value (10,000 dollars)	增长 （%） Increase Rate (%)	占全市比重 （%） Proportion of the whole city values (%)
西安市 Xi'an	396.96	24.6	—	247800	23.6	—
新城区 Xincheng District	26.99	27.1	11.6	7800	15.3	13.4
碑林区 Beilin District	33.03	18.8	14.2	7800	24.3	13.4
莲湖区 Lianhu District	34.74	18.8	15.0	7800	5.3	13.4
灞桥区 Baqiao District	16.85	24.3	7.3	7397	23.3	12.7
未央区 Weiyang District	25.00	27.5	10.8	7800	25.8	13.4
雁塔区 Yanta District	34.50	24.5	14.9	8190	18.5	14.1
阎良区 Yanliang District	8.09	24.4	3.5	2200	6.3	3.8
临潼区 Lintong District	8.01	27.9	3.5	2400	20.0	4.1
长安区 Chang'an District	24.72	35.0	10.7	2768	20.3	4.8
蓝田县 Lantian County	2.67	25.9	1.2	1100	1.0	1.9
周至县 Zhouzhi County	2.10	35.4	0.9	650	8.3	1.1
户　县 Huxian County	5.58	24.6	2.4	1100	4.8	1.9
高陵县 Gaoling County	9.53	36.1	4.1	1115	5.2	1.9

2012年全市各区县经济社会主要指标（续4）
Main Economic and Social Index for Xi'an Districts and Counties in 2012(Continue Ⅳ)

名 称 Name	城镇居民人均可支配收入 Per Capita disposable income for urban residents		农村居民家庭人均纯收入 Net income for rural residents	
	绝对额 （亿元） Absolute Value (100 million yuan)	增长 （%） Increase Rate (%)	绝对额 （亿元） Absolute Value (100 million yuan)	增长 （%） Increase Rate (%)
西安市 Xi'an	29982	15.4	11442	16.9
新城区 Xincheng District	30658	15.7	–	–
碑林区 Beilin District	31268	15.7	–	–
莲湖区 Lianhu District	31195	15.7	–	–
灞桥区 Baqiao District	28688	15.6	13278	17.6
未央区 Weiyang District	30103	15.6	14562	17.6
雁塔区 Yanta District	31934	15.7	14800	17.6
阎良区 Yanliang District	31026	15.6	13403	17.3
临潼区 Lintong District	24568	15.5	10685	17.3
长安区 Chang'an District	26493	15.6	11107	17.9
蓝田县 Lantian County	19957	15.3	7824	16.7
周至县 Zhouzhi County	20025	15.4	7733	16.9
户　县 Huxian County	22520	15.3	9654	16.8
高陵县 Gaoling County	23462	15.5	10673	17.9

前景目标
Prospects and Targets

2013年发展目标
Development target for 2013

远景展望
Prospects

2013年发展目标

- 地区生产总值增长12.5%左右
- 规模以上工业增加值增长16%
- 全社会固定资产投资增长25%左右
- 社会消费品零售总额增长16%以上
- 地方财政一般预算收入增长17%
- 城镇居民人均可支配收入增长14%
- 农村居民人均纯收入增长15%

Development target for 2013

- GDP shall increase by 12.5%
- Added Value of above-scale industries shall increase by 16%
- Investment in social fixed assets shall increase by 25%
- Retail sales of social consumption shall increase by 16%
- Local revenue shall increase by 17%
- Per Capita disposable income for urban residents shall increase by 14%
- Per Capita net income for rural residents shall increase by 15%

远景展望

● 到2016年，优势产业支撑带动作用明显增强，文化建设成效明显，生态环境持续改善，社会管理安全有序，城市交通拥堵有效缓解，人民生活水平大幅提升，地区生产总值达到8000亿元，在西部地区率先实现全面小康社会，国际化主要指标有较大提高，一些优势领域基本达到国际化城市的水平，初步形成国际化大都市的基本框架；

● 到2030年，在综合实力、市场体系、基础设施功能、城市管理、生态建设、人居环境、国际影响力等方面显著提高，建成彰显华夏文明的历史文化基地、国际一流旅游目的地城市，初步建成特色鲜明、功能基本齐备的国际化大都市；

● 到2050年，全面实现建设具有历史文化特色的国际化大都市的目标。

Prospects

- We will work hard to achieve the following goals by 2016 that the advantageous industries shall be greatly enhanced, cultural industry shall make notable achievements, ecological environment shall be significantly improved, social management shall be orderly secured urban traffic and transportation problems shall be effectively relieved, the GDP shall reach 800 billion yuan. Xi'an shall be built into a leading well-off society in an all-round way in western region, with major internationalization indexes raised and some advantageous industries meeting the international standard, and therefore form the basic framework of international metropolis.
- We shall work hard to ensure that, by the year of 2030, significant development shall be made in our comprehensive strength, market system, infrastructure function, urban management, ecological environment, living environment for residents, international influence and so on. Xi'an will be built into a showcase of Chinese civilization and world-class tourist destination, as well as an international metropolis at an initial stage with distinctive features and relative complete urban functions.
- By 2050, Xi'an shall be built into an international metropolis with cultural and historical features.

图书在版编目（CIP）数据

西安概览 / 中共西安市委办公厅，西安市人民政府办公厅编. —4版. —西安：西安出版社，2013.4
ISBN 978-7-80712-125-1

Ⅰ．①中… Ⅱ．①西… Ⅲ．①西安市—概况 Ⅳ．①K924.11

中国版本图书馆CIP数据核字（2013）第063009号

2013 西安概览

编　　著:	中共西安市委办公厅
	西安市人民政府办公厅
出版发行:	西安出版社
社　　址:	西安市长安北路56号
电　　话:	(029) 85234619
邮政编码:	710061
印　　刷:	西安奇良海德印刷有限公司
开　　本:	787mm×1092mm　1/32
印　　张:	3
字　　数:	72千
版　　次:	2013年4月第5版
	2013年4月第1次印刷
ISBN 978-7-80712-125-1	
定　　价:	20.00元

本书如有缺页、误装，请寄回另换。